Freaky Facts about Mummies

MINNETONKA, MINNESOTA

Text and illustrations copyright © 2006 by Two-Can Publishing

Two-Can Publishing
11571 K-Tel Drive
Minnetonka, MN 55343
www.two-canpublishing.com

Written by Iqbal Hussain
illustrated by Andrew Peters
Edited by Jill Anderson
Cover design and Mac production by Joe Fahey

Many thanks to Dr. Arthur Aufderheide, professor of pathology and laboratory medicine at the University of Minnesota–Duluth, for lending his considerable expertise on mummies.

Photographs:
Cover: © Ira Block/National Geographic Image Collection/Getty Images; pp. 4–5, 8–9 (both), 10, 12, 13: Copyright © the Trustees of The British Museum; p. 6 (background): © Author's Image/Matton Images; pp. 6 (mummy), 26, 28, 30: © Corbis/Sygma; pp. 10–11: Anthropoid cartonnage containing mummy of Shepenmut, Priestess of Thebes, NO_DATA/ © Royal Albert Memorial Museum, Exeter, Devon, UK/Bridgeman Art Library; pp. 14–15: © SIME/Corbis; p. 17: © The Egyptian Museum, Turin, Italy/Werner Forman Archive; pp. 18–19: © bygonetimes/Alamy; p. 19 (top): Elvele Images/Alamy; pp. 20–21: Courtesy of Advertising Archives; pp. 22–23: © Moesgård Museum; p. 23 (top): © Science Photo Library; p. 24: © Greenland National Museum & Archives; p. 27: © William Albert Allard/National Geographic Image Collection; p. 31: © Rex Features.

Library of Congress Cataloging-in-Publication Data on file

ISBN 1-58728-537-1 (HC)
ISBN 1-58728-538-X (PB)

Printed in China

1 2 3 4 5 10 09 08 07 06

What's Inside

What Is a Mummy?

Mummies are dead bodies that have survived for thousands of years. All kinds of strange mummies—from people to pets—have been found all over the world. Each mummy tells its own fascinating story about the past.

How Are Mummies Made?

The body of a mummy does not rot because it has been specially preserved. Sometimes bodies are mummified by accident, like when they are frozen in a block of ice. But most mummies are still around because their bodies were handled in a special way to keep them from decomposing.

BOG WOMAN

DRIED-UP MAN

ICE MAN

No Preservatives

For bodies to mummify naturally, the weather needs to be just right. In Egypt and China, the scorching desert heat has dried up bodies in the sand. In Northern Europe, a few mummies have been perfectly preserved in wet, marshy bogs.

HEE HEE!

Where do mummies go for a swim? The Dead Sea!

HA HA!

What's in a Name?

The name "mummy" comes from the Arabic word "mummiya," which means tar. Lots of mummies have been discovered with a tar-like coating on their bandages.

Why Make Mummies?

Many ancient cultures believed that when a person died, he or she would start an exciting life in a strange new world. This was called the afterlife. It was thought that they would need their bodies in the other world, so they were made into mummies. The mummies were buried with food, drinks, and other items they might want or need in their new life.

▲ At more than 5,000 years old, this mummy's a real old-timer. Discovered in a shallow sandy grave in the Egyptian desert, he was nicknamed Ginger because of the color of his hair.

Land of the Mummies

▲ Ramses II ruled Egypt 3,000 years ago. His mummy is so well preserved that you can still tell what he looked like.

A GRAVE PLACE

Over 4,000 years ago, ancient Egypt became the world's number one mummy hot spot. This vast land was ruled by powerful kings called pharaohs. The pharoahs wanted their bodies to be preserved forever. So people set to work to find a way.

Stop the Rot!

Before the ancient Egyptians started making mummies, they buried dead bodies in sandpits, where they would slowly rot away. But the pharoahs wanted to look their best in the afterlife. So Egyptians developed a process called embalming, which kept bodies from rotting. The pharoahs built huge huge pyramids to hold their bodies.

Pharaohs First

At first, only pharaohs were made into mummies, but soon the craze spread across the land. Rich people paid a fortune to become highly decorated mummies, while the poor just got a basic makeover.

Strange but True

Police experts at Scotland Yard, in England, have the fingerprints of an Egyptian mummy in their records!

Mummy-Makers

People who made mummies were called embalmers. They had the rather disgusting job of turning dead bodies into objects that could last forever. Each body took a long time to prepare. Most Egyptians were made into mummies, so you can imagine how busy the embalmers were!

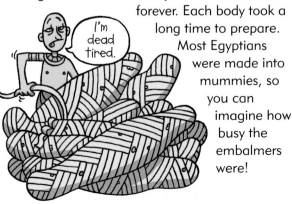

Cracking the Code

In 1798, the French emperor Napoleon led an expedition to Egypt. He brought scientists with him to study ancient Egyptian monuments, mummies' tombs, and a strange kind of picture-writing called hieroglyphs. No one could understand the hieroglyphs until one of the Frenchmen made an amazing discovery.

One day, an officer in Napoleon's army found a stone at a place called Rosetta, near the Nile River. The stone was half-buried and covered in strange writing.

What's this old thing?

There were three kinds of writing on the stone, one of which was Greek. It took Jean-François Champollion, a French scholar, 15 years to figure out what it meant.

He cracked the code, allowing scientists to read messages found in the mummies' tombs.

The treasure is in the... aaagh!

Wrap and Roll

So what did embalmers do to make a body last thousands of years? Well, it was a smelly and messy job that took about 70 days. The work usually included reciting spells to protect the mummy as it made its journey into the afterlife.

HOW TO MAKE A MUMMY

1 First cut open the body and take out all the internal organs, including the heart. Then pull out the brain through the nose.

3 After 40 days, stuff the body with linen, leaves, or sawdust. Then put the heart back in and place round stones in the eye sockets.

2 Next, wash the body with wine or vinegar. Pack natron (a kind of salt) around it and leave it to dry.

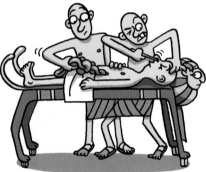

amulet

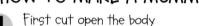

4 Rub lots of oils and spices into the body to keep the skin from drying and cracking.

5 Spend 15 days wrapping the body in bandages. Don't forget to slip a few charms in between the layers.

Strange but True

One mummy was wrapped in 3 miles (4.8 km) of bandages. That's enough to go around a football field 15 times!

Insides Out!

Are you wondering what happened to those internal organs left lying on the table? Well, they were stuffed into specially decorated pots called canopic jars and buried in the tomb with the mummy.

Mummy Makeover

As a finishing touch, the mummy's face was covered with a painted mask. Some masks showed what a person looked like before he or she died, but usually the mask was much more beautiful than the real face.

▲ Here's a completely wrapped mummy. It's covered with a top wrapping called a shroud. An embalmer has placed an amulet, or charm, over the heart for good luck.

All Boxed Up

Painted cases for mummies were very popular with wealthy Egyptians. The mummies of poor Egyptians were either buried in a simple box or put straight into the ground.

Safe and Sound

The first mummy cases were long and rectangular. They looked plain but offered some protection against robbers. These people made a living by stealing jewelry and amulets that were often buried with mummies.

How many more to go?

All Shapes and Sizes

Later, mummy cases were given a new look and shaped with a head, shoulders, and feet. If you were rich, you could even be buried in lots of cases that fitted inside one another, just like Russian dolls.

Strange but True

Often, coffins were decorated with painted doors, so that the mummy's spirit could come and go when it felt like it!

Keeping a Lookout

Many mummy cases had spells painted on them to ward off evil. Some coffins even had spooky fake eyes painted on them, so that the mummy could see out. If anything terrible happened to the body, Egyptians figured that the dead person's spirit could use the case for a body.

Who's watching who?

Cry-Babies

When it came time to bury the mummy, the show really began. Women were hired to cry and wail at the funerals of rich people. While the mummy was buried, mourners beat their chests, pulled their hair, and even flung soil over themselves.

This mummy case belongs to a priestess called Shepenmut. A goddess spreads her wings across the case, protecting the mummy inside.

Pet Mummies

People weren't the only ones in ancient Egypt who got the mummy treatment. Pets were made into mummies too. There was room for millions of happy animals in the afterlife!

Check out my beautiful wrappings!

Beastly Disguise

All kinds of creatures were bandaged up—fish, birds, and even snakes! They were made into mummies because the ancient Egyptians thought that many animals were really gods in disguise.

Help! I can't get out.

Sticky Business

A few unlucky creatures ended up as mummies by accident. Flies came to a sticky end by falling into a hot resin that was poured over the mummy's body. And small lizards were sometimes trapped between the bandages.

Holy Cow!

One kind of bull, called the Apis, was thought to be sacred. This bull lived a life of total luxury—he even had servants! When the bull died, it was mummified and buried in a style fit for a pharaoh. It had a stone coffin, called a sarcophagus, that weighed more than a truck.

That's Weird

Even ferocious crocodiles were made into mummies. These were sacred reptiles that lived at the temples. Visitors fed them meat and wine and dressed them in expensive gold jewelry!

I'm purrfectly wrapped!

The Case for Cats

The ancient Egyptians were crazy about cats. When pet cats died, their owners shaved off their their own eyebrows as a way of mourning their loss. Then they mummified the cats and buried them in cat-shaped cases, so that they would see them again in the afterlife.

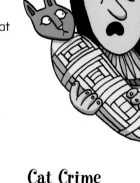

Cat Crime

It wasn't a good idea to pester an ancient Egyptian cat. The Egyptians believed that cats were sacred, and if anyone was caught harming one, he or she could be sentenced to death. The cats that lived around temples were particularly lucky. People brought food and milk to honor these fortunate felines.

▲ Cat mummies were often given expressions. This one is smiling.

Home Sweet Pyramid

The pharaohs made sure that they would live in luxury even after they died. They had enormous pyramids built to hold their tombs. The tombs were often decorated with beautiful pictures and hieroglyphs.

Take-Away Treasure

The first pharaohs had their bodies laid to rest in chambers deep inside pyramids. These rooms were filled with gold, jewels, and other treasures. There were also useful items such as clothes, food, and furniture. And for rainy days in the afterlife, there were even games!

▲ These giant pyramids at Giza in Egypt were built by the early pharaohs. They are about 4,500 years old.

That's Weird

The Egyptians believed that the sloping sides of a pyramid represented the slanting rays of the sun. The spirit of a pharaoh used the rays to climb up to heaven.

A few of the early pharaohs had a gruesome solution to taking it easy in the next world. They had their servants killed and buried with them!

Later, pharaohs were buried with hundreds of small statues called shabtis. People believed these statues would magically come to life in the afterlife and step up to serve their master.

Tomb Raiders

Every Egyptian, including robbers, knew that the pyramids were piled high with tempting treasures. The pharaohs tried to make their pyramids burglar-proof, but they didn't succeed.

PYRAMID PESTS

Treasure Trail

The Book of Buried Pearls was a step-by-step guide to tomb raiding. It gave would-be thieves lists of hidden treasures, maps showing where to find the goodies, and spells to outwit the guardian spirits inside the tombs.

Off with Their Heads!

The tomb robbers were often the workers who had helped to build the tombs in the first place. With a little help, they could find the treasure, sell it, and settle down to a life of luxury. But if they were caught, they were tortured or even executed.

Get your death mask here.

TRICKING THIEVES

That'll fool them.

Pyramid builders tried to fool thieves by sealing the entrance with a mighty slab of stone.

If robbers got in, then they had to find their way through a maze of tunnels, dead ends, and deep pits.

Aaaaaaargh!

I'm almost there!

Robbers chipped away at the walls. Just when they thought they'd found the treasure ... a huge stone blocked the way!

End of the Pyramids

Eventually, the pharaohs became so fed up with pyramid-robbing that they hatched a new plan. Instead of building pyramids, they had secret tombs cut into the cliffs of a desert valley called the Valley of the Kings. For a while, the mummies and their possessions were safe. But soon the thieves caught on and the looting began again.

Mummy Medicine

Treasure was not the only reason for tomb raiding. Mummies had their uses, too. In 17th-century England, people thought that powdered mummy was a magical healing potion. They rubbed it into their skin or swallowed it like medicine.

Full Steam Ahead!

Legend has it that mummies were once used as fuel, because their wrappings burned well. A story written in the 1860s claimed that trains in Egypt were powered by the burning of mummies.

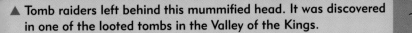

▲ Tomb raiders left behind this mummified head. It was discovered in one of the looted tombs in the Valley of the Kings.

The World's Most Famous Mummy

Slow and Steady

Howard Carter was a real slowpoke. He spent ten years searching for the tomb. Then he took eight years to clear out over 5,000 objects, and another ten years to list them all in detail. Carter was so thorough and patient that he didn't even open the first coffin until almost three years after he had found it!

Thieves made off with lots of loot from the Valley of the Kings, but they missed the grand prize—the tomb of King Tutankhamen. When this hideaway was discovered by Howard Carter in 1922, it had not been opened for 3,000 years.

Zzzzzzzzz.

Golden Goodies

Inside King Tut's tomb, there were piles of golden objects, including necklaces, bracelets, thrones, chariots, tables, statues, swords, and shields. There were also about 100 pairs of shoes, 30 boomerangs, ostrich feather fans, trumpets, and a first-aid kit.

98...99...

The King's Case

Tutankhamen was a young pharaoh who died when he was about 20 years old. He was buried inside three beautiful, decorated cases, which fit snugly one inside another. The smallest case was made of solid gold.

Behind the Mask

Tutankhamen's mummy wore a glittering gold mask, studded with semi-precious stones. It weighed more than 22 pounds (10 kg). The mask was so firmly stuck to Tutankhamen's head that scientists had to slide hot knives underneath it to pry it off.

Strange but True

Tutankhamen collected earrings. Inside his tomb, there were several pairs to wear in the afterlife.

This is the second of Tut's three classy cases. But the face on this case is different from the others. Was it made for someone else?

The Mummy's Curse

It seems that there was a price to pay for disturbing Tutankhamen. Several people connected with the discovery of the tomb died soon afterwards. Rumors spread that they were victims of a 3,000-year-old curse!

Lordy, Lordy

Lord Carnarvon was victim number one. He had paid for Howard Carter's research, and he was one of the first to enter Tut's tomb. Five months later, he died from a mosquito bite on his cheek. The moment he died, all the lights in Cairo went out. Back in England, his dog dropped dead!

Get Carter

If there was a curse, Howard Carter should have been first in line for punishment. After all, he'd been the one to break into Tut's tomb! But he dismissed reports of the curse as "ridiculous stories." He lived on for many more years, until his death in March 1939—from natural causes.

FEAR

"T

MU

ALL NEW!
IN TERRIFYING
TECHNICOLO

Mummies in the Movies

A curse makes for a great story, and Hollywood loved the idea of a mummy seeking revenge from beyond the grave. In 1932, Boris Karloff starred in *The Mummy*, the first in a long line of horror movies featuring bandaged zombies. Karloff based his creepy look on a real mummy of an ancient Egyptian pharaoh, Tuthmosis III.

That's Weird

On the day that Tut's tomb was opened, Carter's pet canary was gobbled up by a giant cobra. Big deal, huh—except that Tut's mummy mask has a cobra on its forehead!

▲ Mummies became the spooky inspiration for many films made in Hollywood during the 1930s and 1940s.

Bog Mummies

Across Northern Europe, nearly 2,000 ancient bodies have been discovered in murky peat bogs and marshes. Some of the bodies are so well preserved that archaeologists can even take their fingerprints.

How did I end up lying here?

Mistaken Identity

In 1952, gruesome Grauballe Man was found in a bog in Denmark. Local people thought he was a man who had disappeared 70 years earlier, after a rowdy night out. Later they discovered that the mummy was 1,500 years old.

▲ Grauballe Man ate his supper before he fell into his watery grave. The scientists who examined his body discovered wheat, rye, and weed seeds swimming around inside his stomach. Mmm, tasty!

A Deep Sleep

The circumstances surrounding Tollund Man's death were more suspicious. This 2,000-year-old sleeping beauty was found in a dreary bog in Denmark—with a leather noose around his neck! Archaeologists think that Tollund Man was probably hanged as a sacrifice to the gods.

Hey, great tan!

Getting a Tan

When Lindow Man was hauled out of a moist peat bog in England in 1984, he looked like he had spent his life on a sun-drenched beach in the Bahamas. Acid in the peat had given him an all-over tan and turned his skin to leather.

Manicured Mummy

Archaeologists carefully studied Lindow Man for clues to his identity. They figured out that he was about 25 years old when he died. His hands were smooth and his fingernails were neat, which meant that he hadn't done much heavy work. He may have held an important position in his village.

Ice Mummies

If you're planning on making a mummy, take a quick trip to icy lands in the north of the world. There, you can freeze-dry a body in the chilly air or make your own human popsicle in a block of ice.

Dressed to Chill

This mummy of a tiny Inuit boy was buried in the snow in Greenland. His relatives had dressed him up in a cozy fur parka, thick pants, and padded boots to keep out the bitter cold as he trekked into the next world.

Believe It or Not
Once, a freeze-dried chicken was discovered behind the walls of a house in England.

THE ICEMAN

Around 3000 B.C., a traveler was hiking high in the Alps in Italy. At some point, he ran into trouble.

Now where is that urgent-care clinic?

Injured by an arrow in his back, he struggled to keep going. But his injury and the weather were too much.

The man died, and his body was frozen. He was covered in snow for 5,000 years until two hikers found him in 1991.

Let's call him Iceman.

Mummies in the Freezer

In 1993, archaeologists in Russia unearthed a magnificent tomb from the cold, windswept land of Siberia. The tomb belonged to the ancient Pazyryk people and was hidden far below the ground. Rainwater had seeped into the tomb and turned it into a giant deep freezer.

mummified horses

stone cover

man in shallow coffin

log chamber

woman in carved coffin

food and drink to enjoy in the afterlife

All Dressed Up

Inside the icy tomb, everything was perfectly preserved. A man rested in a shallow coffin on the roof, while a woman slept below. She must have been wealthy and important. She was clothed in luxurious furs and wore a wooden headdress carved with cats and swans and covered in gold. Her shoulders and wrists were tattooed with pictures of amazing beasts.

Ice mummies hate warm weather! When their frozen bodies are taken from their chilly tombs, they soon begin to melt. Within a few days, the warm temperatures make a creeping, smelly fungus grow on the mummies!

ICE CREAM

FROZEN PIZZA

MUMMIES

Scientists store mummies in giant refrigerators to keep them fresh. The mummies are taken out only on special occasions, and then just for short periods.

Odd-Ball
Mummies

Mummies turn up all over the place. Each one has its own unique style, from a well-dressed body lying in a coffin to a seated corpse in a cloth bundle.

Dead-Heads

In the past, the Chimu people of Peru gave their dead false heads. When family members died, they were hung out in the sun to dry. Then, relatives squashed them into a cloth bundle and made them fake heads. Wigs of human hair, shell eyes, and feather eyelashes were added as a final touch.

Nice eyelashes!

Mystery Man of China

One mummy discovery gave archaeologists a real headache. Determined investigators uncovered an ancient tomb in China, but the three bodies inside it, including the man above, were not Chinese. Instead, they came from a tribe from Europe. No one knows how they ended up in China.

A Date with the Dead

Did you know that a few people used to have lunch with mummies? In Palermo, Sicily, 2,000 mummies and 6,000 skeletons are stored in an underground tomb. Their living relatives used to bring picnics to the tomb and chat with the mummies as if they were alive.

> Pass the pizza, please.

Ruling Bodies

When a ruler of the ancient South American Inca people died, his subjects dried his body in the cool mountain air. They treated the mummy as though it were still their leader, and brought it food and drink every day. They even took it on day trips to visit other mummies!

How to Get a Head!

The native Jivaro people of South America used to chop off an enemy's head and plop it into boiling hot water. Then they stuffed the shrunken head with hot sand. These steps made the head shrink to the size of a man's fist. The shrunken head was worn as a necklace during festivals, in hopes that the dead person's strength would pass to the wearer.

> Two heads are better than one!

Mummy Detectives

Being a mummy detective is a gruesome but great job. Scientists study mummies to find out how people lived long ago, what clothes they wore, and even how they died.

▲ This mangled mummy was a Siberian warrior. By looking at his skin and bones, scientists can figure out the kinds of injuries he suffered in battle.

That's Weird

In England in the 1800s, the unwrapping of a mummy was a special event that drew big crowds. Surgeons carried out the honors before an amazed audience, sometimes using a hammer and chisel to remove the hardened bandages.

Open Wide!

A mummy's mouth can tell you a lot. By looking at the teeth, you can tell how old the person was when he or she died. You can also find out a mummy's favorite meal. Worn teeth show that the mummy's daily bread was full of sand and grit!

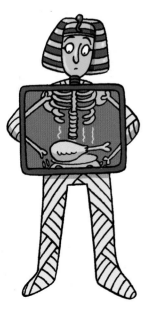

Tools of the Trade

When studying a mummy, scientists may take samples of the skin and bone. They can tell if the person had any germs or diseases when he or she was alive. And with X-ray machines, scientists can take pictures of a mummy's insides. By studying the contents of a mummy's stomach, they can figure out what the mummy ate for its last meal.

Tell Me Why

RAMSES II NEEDED A PASSPORT

In 1974, horrified scientists discovered that the mummy of the pharaoh Ramses II had a weird skin infection. The mummy was flown to Paris for tests. He was given a passport which listed his job as "King (deceased)"!

Luckily, scientists in Paris were able to cure him quickly. While examining his body, they also learned that the clever Egyptian embalmers had stuffed Ramses' nose with peppercorns to keep its hooked shape.

29

Mummy Hall of Fame

Ready to meet some of the spookiest and most amazing mummies of all? They're all here, in the mummy hall of fame.

Fishy Tale

Mummies don't come any stranger than this. One man tried to trick the world into believing that he had found a mummified merman—the half-man, half-fish creature from old sea legends. He took the head of a monkey and tail of a fish and joined them together to make a mummy.

Are you for real?

Loveliest Lady

This lady, nicknamed the Loulan Beauty, wins the beauty contest for mummies. Discovered in China in 1980, she became world-famous for her lovely face and long hair. Artists have even painted pictures of how they think she looked before she died.

King of Cool

Hello, Gramps!

The coolest mummy must be the Iceman. He's so ancient that he had already been frozen for almost 1,000 years when the ancient Egyptian pharaohs were being buried. Old Iceman still looks pretty good for his age!

Waxy Wonder

One of the most popular—and eerily life-like—mummies is the Russian leader Vladimir Lenin. His body was mummified in 1924, using a top-secret wax process. Since then, thousands have come to see it every day. Now some people want to have him buried with other officials from Russia's old Communist government.

Mummy Molds

In the year 79, a volcano in Italy called Vesuvius erupted. Over 2,000 people and animals in the nearby city of Pompeii were buried alive under a blanket of hot ash.

The dead bodies rotted away, leaving behind hollows in the hardened ash. Archaeologists have poured liquid plaster into the hollows, making mummy-like molds that reveal the frightening last moments of these people's lives.

Mountain Maiden

This Inca girl is the tops! Her mummified body was found an incredible 20,700 feet (6,300 m) above sea level, on top of a volcano in the Andes Mountains of South America. Experts believe she was put there as a gift to the mountain gods.

Tricky Words

afterlife: the perfect world entered after death, according to Ancient Egyptian beliefs

archaeologist (ar-kee-ALL-uh-jist): a person who learns about the past by studying old buildings and ancient remains

bog: an area of soft, wet ground. Many preserved bodies have been found in bogs in Northern Europe.

embalm: to preserve a body using chemicals and lotions

hieroglyphs (HY-ro-gliffs): a form of writing used by the ancient Egyptians, which uses pictures to represent objects, ideas, and sounds

mummify: to turn into a mummy, either naturally or by embalming

pharaoh (FAIR-o): an ancient Egyptian ruler, or king

sacred: something that has special religious meaning and importance

tomb (TOOM): a building or room where dead bodies are placed

Index